THE FORMULA

Your Guide to Building an Impactful Brand

Hey Yolanda! Thank you so much for your support! ♥ Bran.

By:

Briana Ross

www.brianaross.co

Dedication

This is for my late great-grandmother Sarah, thank you so much for believing in me and always encouraging me to dream bigger.

To my husband Kenneth and our daughters Bailee and Alaina, thank you so much for your love and support. You guys are my world.

TABLE OF CONTENTS

INTRODUCTION

Hi!

My name is Briana Ross! I'm a Brand Strategist, Graphic Designer, Speaker, and owner of HelloBriana Consulting. I teach entrepreneurs how to build impactful brands that align with their target audience and create valuable content that resonates with them.

Over the past three years in business, I noticed the biggest struggles for my clients were bringing their visions to life and actually growing their brands. They had spent hundreds and even thousands on marketing, but they were not getting an ROI (Return On Investment). It wasn't because their product or service was lacking, but they were missing a key component required for longevity.

Many of us start a business and immediately start marketing our products and services without defining our target audience and building a relationship with them. Unfortunately, this vital misstep can lead to us addressing the wrong audience. Then we get frustrated and even consider quitting because we're unable to figure out what we're doing wrong. The answer is pretty simple.

Your branding is off. . .

Often when we think of branding, we automatically think of colors and logos. While this is a part of branding, it only makes up a small portion. Branding is how you want people to feel when they come in contact with your business.

When you're clear on the problem you solve for people, you can then begin to understand who your product or service is for, their goals and challenges, and how your solution will fit into their daily lives. Once you're clear on those areas, you can then begin to create a visual brand strategy that attracts them, and you know what colors, fonts, and other visual elements they prefer.

When you have a solid brand strategy in place, you can then build a relationship with your target audience and market your business with confidence. Yes, you're in business because you're doing something you love; however, you have to remember that your product or service needs to solve a problem. If you're not clear on the problem you solve for your customers or clients, then you will struggle to find your target audience, which leads to not getting consistent results in your business. You have amazing products and services; you need to package it correctly so you can attract your target audience.

In this guide, I'm going to teach you how to do just that. You're going to learn the exact formulas that I've used to build my own brand and help hundreds of entrepreneurs do the same.

PART ONE
You Can, and You Will

Before we dive into branding, I want to share a little bit about myself. I want you to have a clear vision of who I am, why I am so passionate about what I do, and the things I have been able to accomplish in my business. We will discuss more in detail why this is so important later in this guide.

I knew I wanted to be a business owner at a young age, but I had no idea how or when that would happen. I realized as an adult that babysitting at 13 spearheaded my journey into the entrepreneurial world. I had the chance to choose when I babysat, set my own prices, and pick who I wanted to work with. That's something many of us aim to do now as entrepreneurs.

If you would've told me five years ago, I would now be a full-time business owner consistently making four-figures a month and doing something I love; I probably wouldn't have believed you. Not because I didn't think I could do it, but I just didn't see anything like that happening so soon. I was a newlywed with no kids and living a pretty comfortable life working as a guest services representative at a world-renown hotel. My husband and I found out we were expecting our first child, and my life began to change drastically. I no longer wanted to work crazy hours, and I had a strong desire for more flexibility. Fortunately, I landed an at-home customer service position that allowed me to set my own schedule. This was my first taste of freedom. While working at this job at home, my mind began to wonder. I started to ask questions like:

- How can I make more money?

- How can I make money while spending more time with my daughter?

- Is it possible to make money consistently online?

After doing some research, I realized my experience in customer service, sales, and management equipped me with the knowledge that many entrepreneurs don't have easy access to. I've always wanted to help people, and I've always wanted to teach (I even studied childhood development for a while), so why not teach entrepreneurs how to build their businesses based on what I learned working for larger corporations.

I didn't start teaching brand strategy right away. I had to do a lot of testing and learning. I had to be ok with things not going as planned, and be flexible because things are always changing. I was really confused starting, but as I tested ideas out and took action, I got closer to where I wanted to be. That's the thing about entrepreneurship, you may not always have things figured out, but as you continue to take steps forward, you'll be that much closer to the answer.

When I first launched HelloBriana Consulting, I was helping entrepreneurs in many different areas, such as customer experience, time management, sales, marketing, and branding. However, I was stretched thin and all over the place. Not only was I stressed out, but I wasn't making any money.

I was in the negative my first year in business because of the money I put into it. After a lesson filled first year in business, I knew my second year had to be totally different. As I continued to work from home while building my business, we found out we were expecting our second child. This motivated me even more to grow my business and have more time and financial freedom.

I realized if I wanted different results, then I had to do something different. I stepped out of my comfort zone and started going live on Facebook, sharing tips on how to start and grow a business, and the pieces finally began to fall in place. I started getting leads more consistently and realized I'm finally on track to finding my niche.

After investing in a membership, I learned how important it was to have a target audience and define your genius. I felt like I could help everyone, and that was exactly why my business was not growing the way I wanted it to. At the time, I was only offering coaching services and charging very little, but I was ready for growth and ready to make it happen.

I thought about the area most of my clients needed help with, the questions they had, the things I helped them with, the results they got, and the questions I was getting from new entrepreneurs like me, and I realized that everything came back to branding.

Here are the three lessons I learned my first year in business:

· Starting a business requires financial sacrifice to get to the next level, but it doesn't have to break the bank.

· When you try to speak to everyone, no one hears you. You need to have a niche, but sometimes you have to test things out to find your target audience.

· You have to test things out to figure out what works and what doesn't work, so don't stress perfection.

My second year in business was quite the rollercoaster. It started on a high as we welcomed our second daughter. By this time, I was offering graphic design services after declining many requests, and maternity leave gave me the flexibility to test out this new service. I was able to take two months off from work, so during that time, I focused on building my graphic design portfolio. As I was preparing to go back to work, tragedy struck. My great-grandmother passed away. She was my best friend, inspiration, and so much more. She also helped me out a lot with my daughters. I was blessed not to have to pay for daycare and be able to have the freedom to network and attend events.

Just weeks before she had passed away, I had just hosted my first event and had my first speaking engagement. Now, I was faced with an even tougher decision. Return to work and spend hundreds on daycare (which would have been half of my paycheck), or take the risk and focus on my business full-time. With the amazing support of my husband, I decided to go for it. Talk about a strain. Times were not easy because I had not yet supplemented my income, but something changed. Although I felt like I was losing myself dealing with the loss of my grandma, my business began to grow like a wildflower. Not many knew how hurt I was because I used the pain of losing my grandmother to fuel my business. After all, she was the first person to believe in my business. Even when I had trouble believing in myself, she did, and to this day, she still inspires and motivates me.

I knew if I wanted to grow my brand, I had to get out there and network. I quickly recognized my strength of public speaking, which led to me booking speaking engagements, hosting events, and networking more. I also began offering more online resources teaching entrepreneurs how to build impactful brands. This included blogs, Facebook groups, online courses, ebooks, and other online resources.

During my second year, I finally surpassed the amount I was making while working from home. My business finally began to profit, and I was finally working with the amazing women I dreamed about working with.

My second year in business taught me three key things:

- Our time here on Earth is limited, so be sure to spend time with the ones you love and make memories.

- Take action, and do it scared! Growth lies where we are often afraid to go.

- Do not be afraid to share your expertise. It is so important to be able to give value because this is what will help set your brand apart from others.

My third year was all about taking what I learned and implementing it into my business. I stopped making excuses, I invested in my brand, and I got clear on how I wanted to serve my audience.

I focused on giving value and teaching entrepreneurs how to build unique experiences around their products and services and helping aspiring authors self-publish their books. I was also able to speak and facilitate workshops in Columbus, Warner Robins, and Atlanta, Georgia, Chicago, and Las Vegas.

Most of us are familiar with the old proverb, 'third time's the charm,' and as I close out my third year in business, I can't help but agree. I finally feel like I have found my groove. Although I have a lot more to learn, I am very pleased with the progress I have made thus far. This past year has been quite the journey.I have been stretched in ways that made me very uncomfortable, and it has been a continuous learning process. However, seeing my dreams start to become a reality is one of the best feelings, and my goal is to help you get the same results.

Building your brand takes time. It's not an overnight process, and you will frequently have to tweak things to make them work for you, but the journey is so worth it. Charge your worth, be selective about who you work with, and learn to say no, because entrepreneurship is stressful and you need to do everything you can to protect your peace.

My third year in business taught me three key things:

- Set boundaries. As an entrepreneur, there is no one telling you when to clock in or out, and you will end up working yourself to death if you do not set boundaries.

- Outsource things you do not want to do. Not only did outsourcing save me a lot of time, but I can make more money because I have help.

- You will not be able to please everyone, and that's ok! This is your journey, so do what you feel is right, and the people who are meant to be there with you will be.

During my time in business, my biggest lesson has been the importance of consistency. Sometimes it's going to feel like nothing is working, and sometimes it will seem like you don't have adequate support. However, you can't let that stop you. This is your journey, and you shouldn't let people dictate how you move and whether or not you chase your dreams.

Remember, you got this, and your hard work will pay off.

No More Excuses; It's Time to Take Action

Before you even dive into this guide, I want you to do a self-assessment.

- How would you rate your mindset?
- Do you know that you can do anything you put your mind to?
- Do you know that you are capable of making, however much money you want?

Believing in yourself is a critical component in building your brand. As cliche as it sounds if you don't believe you won't achieve.
Many of us struggle with our mindsets because of the many ups and downs of entrepreneurship. Most will experience not having someone to share their goals and struggles with.

We get so caught up in what everyone else is doing, and we let social media psyche us out of our greatness. WHY do we do that? Because we've allowed social media to make us believe everything on social media is real.

The thing is, social media is exaggerated; what you see isn't the entire story. Many of us only post the glitz and glamours of our lives because we're too afraid of letting people see what life is like for us. There's nothing wrong with being private, but it does create a fake persona, which in return can make it hard to build your brand. No one is perfect. We are all facing many different battles daily, but that's what makes life beautiful. NO ONE has it all together, so stop putting so much pressure on yourself.

You can build a business that stands out even though there are many businesses out there that offer a similar product or service. There's enough room for everybody, including you. When you learn to believe in yourself, the unimaginable will begin to happen. Ask, and ye shall receive, manifest your desires, you get what you put out into the universe, or however else you want to put it; ultimately, if you want it you can have it.

However, you can't just want or ask for something, then sit and wait. You have to be ready and willing to put in the work to obtain it. That's usually the reason why a lot of us get so discouraged. We know what we want, but we expect it to be delivered on a silver platter. It's time to stop making excuses and do the work. Understand that you were built for this journey. Your amazing ideas weren't put in your head for no reason. Those big dreams of living a financially free life with no worries aren't unrealistic. You need to have a plan in place and be ready and willing to go through difficult trials, so you can make it happen.

One of the many things that have helped improve my mindset is journaling. I originally started writing when I was very young, but I stopped for years during my adult years. I felt as though I had nothing to write about, and I felt like I didn't have enough time.

I made every excuse in the book as to why I wasn't doing what I loved anymore, but one day I was down in the dumps, and the only thing I could think to do was write. Writing has always been therapeutic for me, so making the time to start doing it again changed my life. Not only did I journal, but I would write three positive things that happened that day and three things I was grateful for. Talk about a shift! Because I focused my energy on what I was grateful for, the things I desired started to come more easily.

Stop focusing on what you don't have, and pay attention to the blessing right in front of you. If you want something, write it down or say it to put it out there, then begin working on a plan to accomplish it. When I read where I was a year ago, I was truly amazed because I have come so far. Journaling may not be your thing, but it is a great tool to extend grace and words of affirmation to yourself through this new journey.

If you don't have a lot of time to write, that's ok! I dedicated 15 to 20 minutes each night to write to help me incorporate it into my daily routine. We ALL have 15 to 20 minutes we can spare, and if you want different results, then you have to do something different. Consider adding a mantra(s) and action steps during your journaling time.

Here are some example mantras:

- I am capable of accomplishing anything my heart desires.

- Money is energy, and it flows to me freely.

- I can do this

- This too shall pass

- Anything worth having is worth working hard for

Action Steps

Journal 3 to 5 times a week taking note of the positive things that happen each day and the things you are grateful for.

Start your day with mantras to set the right tone for your day.

Remember, focus on what you already have and be grateful instead of being upset about what you don't have. Your desires will come to fruition; you have to be thankful for how far you've already come.

PART TWO

Your Brand is More Than a Logo

Many times when we think about branding, we think about a business's logo or colors, but branding is so much more than that! Branding is the feeling you want people to have when they come in contact with your business. I will be consistently reminding you that your brand needs to align with your target audience. Questions you'll want to consider include, who are your products and services meant for, what kind of experience do you want your customers or clients to have; and, what do you want them to tell others after doing business with your company? Once you begin to answer those questions, you will have a better idea of how your business should be branded.

Your branding matters immensely. Many of us are struggling in business because of improper branding. Your product or service is excellent, but it tells the wrong story, the message is inconsistent, or it is marketed to the wrong audience. We launch our businesses and begin marketing without even getting to know our audience and building a relationship with them.

Always remember, people, buy things from people they know, like, and trust. You may even be able to get people to buy once without building rapport, but if you want them to be repeated buyers and tell others about your business, then you will have to set yourself apart from other brands. The perfect way to do this is by focusing on giving value and positioning your brand as the go-to brand in your industry.

At 19 years old, I got my first sales job, but it was not easy. I went through a few interviews, and when I was finally hired, my district manager told me, "Briana, I think you have a great personality, but because you don't have any sales experience, I didn't want to hire you. The store manager sees something in you, so don't disappoint. Always remember, people, buy things from people they like." That last sentence changed the game for me. If my customers weren't returning, they were sending people my way. I focused on building a relationship with them, and I genuinely cared. Because I focused on getting to know my customers, I was always one of the top sales representatives in the district each month, and I was offered a management position by the age of 20.

Proper branding will allow you to get in front of your dream customers and clients, become a nationally or even internationally recognized brand, have raving fans who love your brand, and consistently buy from you, and more! Who doesn't want that?!

Your brand strategy is how you will communicate your brand's message and reach your target audience. It's one thing to have a message, but to consistently get results, you need to have a strategy behind how you do that.

Don't stress about having everything together in the beginning. Your brand will evolve. As you work with customers and clients over time, you will have a better idea of who your products and services are for. Business is all about growth and testing things out to see what works and doesn't work. Once you figure out what works, you can then create a system to duplicate results over and over again. You won't have everything together the first time around, and that's ok. The important thing is that you get started with starting or scaling your business.

Remember, don't chase perfection and start where you are now. There are people out there, depending on the products and services you offer. Yes, there may be hundreds if not thousands of brands that offer the same thing or something similar, but there are also billions of people on this Earth, meaning there's plenty of room for you. This isn't a competition to see who's brand launches or scales the fastest, or who's brand makes the most money. This journey is about building a solid foundation for you that will continue to get you results years from now.

Having a brand strategy has allowed me and my clients to launch amazing products and services, consistently make money in our businesses, have four-figure book launches, find and work with dream clients, and so much more. In this guide, I'm going to teach you precisely what I have applied in my business, and what I teach my one-on-one clients.

I'm going to teach you step-by-step how to create a solid brand strategy that aligns with your target audience, will build relationships, and convert them from prospects to leads then paying customers and clients.

Brand Values

The first step to branding your business is setting a solid foundation by having clear brand values, and understanding who exactly your products and services are for. This process is crucial because it helps you determine who your brand is meant for and who it isn't meant for. Believe it or not, your brand isn't for everyone. I know you want to help everyone, and while we may have customers or clients outside of our target audience, you still need to have a target for your branding and, eventually, marketing efforts. Your target audience is your intended audience for your products or services. We will discuss this more in detail later in this guide, but ultimately you want to make sure your target audience has similar values to your brand. In the long run, this will make it easier to communicate and build a relationship with them.

There are three areas you need to define before starting to brand your business in any way, shape, or form visually.

The first area you need to determine is your brand purpose; your why. You should ask yourself questions like why are you in business, why did you choose this specific area of business, and what does this mean to you? It is essential to have a clear why, because almost everything you do leads back to it. When your sales are nonexistent, and you want to quit, you will be taken back to your why. When you have that complicated customer or client who makes you question everything, you will be taken back to your why. When you finally start to crush your income goals, you will be very grateful and remember your why. Your brand purpose is what will get you through the hard times.

Entrepreneurship can sometimes feel like a rollercoaster, and there were many times when I questioned if this was even right for me. Although quitting crossed my mind a few times, I could never bring myself to do it because I knew that entrepreneurship gave me the freedom to spend time with my daughters whenever I wanted, and many entrepreneurs needed my help. I would also think about how far I have come on this journey. Although I wasn't quite where I wanted to be, I still made so much progress. Give yourself credit!

Your brand purpose may be completely different from mine, just as it should be. However, you want to make sure you have a clearly defined why because when the going gets hard, you're going to need that extra push. Make sure your why is an accurate representation of what you want. It shouldn't be for anyone else but you.

The second area you need to define is your brand vision; your what. Your brand vision is where you see your brand in the future.

What type of impact would you like to have? Where do you see your life and business in five to ten years? It is so important to know what you're working towards because this will allow you to move intentionally in your business. Many times when we don't know what next step to take, it's because we don't have clear goals set, and this makes it hard for us actually to move forward. Set goals for your business, so you can create a strategic plan to accomplish them.

Please don't waste any more time doing things to do them; you don't have the time or money to waste. Sometimes we get caught up in the motion and lose sight of our goals and vision. We know what needs to be done, but because we have lost sight of things, we feel confused. If this is you, then revisit your list of goals and determine if you're on or off track.

It's time to be intentional about how you build your brand. I stress setting clear goals and having a clear vision to my clients and audience a lot because, without it, you can't be intentional. Your goals and vision will determine the types of content you share on social media, the brands you partner with, and even the customers and clients you work with. If it doesn't contribute to your end goal, then it doesn't deserve much energy.

The third area you need to be clear on is your brand mission; the how. How will you make an impact? What are you aiming to do? Your brand mission is centered around who you serve and how you serve them. It should clearly define the purpose of your work and the impact you intend to make.

Having a clear brand mission will allow you to create a strategic plan to make your brand vision a reality. What does making an impact means for your brand? How does your product change lives? What amazing results do you help your clients achieve? What sets your brand apart from others? No matter what your product or service is, your brand mission needs to capture who you serve and how you serve them.

When you have a clear brand purpose (why), vision (what), and mission (how), you begin to see who your brand is meant for.

Action Steps

Define your brand values:

Brand Purpose:

_____
_____
_____
_____
_____
_____

Brand Vision:

_____
_____
_____
_____
_____
_____

Brand Mission:

_____
_____
_____
_____
_____
_____

Visualize where you see your business in the next one to five years. Write it down!

_____
_____
_____
_____

What do you want your brand to be known for?

_____

_____

_____

_____

What are three ways you can serve your audience?

_____

_____

_____

_____

_____

_____

_____

_____

_____

_____

_____

_____

Audit & Assess

When building your brand, once you clearly define your brand values, you'll want to audit and assess EVERYTHING. The goal of conducting an audit and assessment is to look at your brand, target audience, and industry. You're going to have to be real with yourself about your strengths and weaknesses when it comes to your business. Consider the things you've done this far to start or grow your brand and think about what worked and what didn't work. To move forward and grow your business, you have to have a clear understanding of where you are now.

Ask yourself questions like:

- Does my brand currently live up to the brand values I outlined?
- Do my current customers and clients align with my brand values?
- Why am I postponing the launch of my brand or a new product or service?
- What have I done so far to start my business?

Brand cohesiveness is required to build a memorable brand, but not just with how things look. Your branding matters when it comes to your message, your voice, your content, how your brand is represented at events, and so much more; think about the people you want to buy your products and services.

Now ask yourself:
- Who are your products and services really for?
- What does your audience like about your current branding? (Don't hesitate to run polls and surveys to find out.)
- What don't they like about it?
- What are some things you have been wanting to do to grow your brand but haven't started?

Consider the feedback you get from your customers and clients. What praises are you getting? What constructive feedback are you getting? This is the time you need to be brutally honest with yourself to ensure that you can offer your customers and clients the best experience possible. Every customer or client won't be happy but always aim to provide the best solution. We have to be honest; things happen, but it's not the end of the world, and you can come back from it.

When thinking about your weaknesses, consider if this is something you can improve, or if this is something you need help with. It's ok to seek advice in your business, and honestly, running a business is not a one-person job. If you're struggling with being consistent with various business tasks, then you may want to consider outsourcing.

Many of us naturally assume outsourcing can be expensive, but there are affordable routes out there. You're missing out on money due to you trying to do everything, so you should strongly consider outsourcing. When I finally started outsourcing tasks in my business, I noticed a huge shift. I had more time to myself, I was able to spend more time with my family, and I made more money because I was able to focus on money-generating activities. If you need help, don't be afraid to go out and get it.

The goal of your brand strategy is to elevate your brand and offer a unique customer experience. Once you understand the strong points and weak points in your brand, you can then create a plan to take things to the next level.

Action Steps

Identify three strengths of your brand

1. _____
   _____
   _____
   _____

2. _____
   _____
   _____
   _____

3. _____
   _____
   _____
   _____

Identify three weaknesses of your brand

1. _____
   _____
   _____
   _____

2. _____
   _____
   _____
   _____

3. _____
   _____
   _____
   _____

Outline three goals you would like to accomplish for your business in the next twelve months:

1. _____
_____
_____
_____

2. _____
_____
_____
_____

3. _____
_____
_____
_____

Identify three things that have been hindering the growth of your brand:

1. _____
_____
_____
_____

2. _____
_____
_____
_____

3. _____
_____
_____
_____

Write three action steps for each block to get around it.

1. _____
   _____
   _____

2. _____
   _____
   _____

3. _____
   _____
   _____

4. _____
   _____
   _____

5. _____
   _____
   _____

6. _____
   _____
   _____

7. _____
   _____
   _____

8. _____
   _____
   _____

9. _____
   _____
   _____

Target Audience, Brand Perception, Market Research

Your target audience is the intended group of people for your products and services. Many people think their products and services are meant for everyone, and while they may be able to work for a wide range of people, it's so important to have a target for your marketing efforts. Marketing to everyone doesn't work because when you try to talk to everyone, no one hears you.

Before we dive in deep, there are some basic things we need to define. When it comes to your target audience, you want to be familiar with their demographics. You can ask yourself questions like:

- How old are they?
- Is your product or service considered a necessity or a luxury?
- Where do they live?
- Do they have disposable income?
- What are their interests?
- What don't they like?

These fundamental questions will help you determine your target audience's demographics. The demographics include but are not limited to gender, age range, household income, and location. This area matters because it determines how you will communicate with your audience and how you will price your products and services.

Then you want to think about their background and daily lives. This includes their job title, what industry they work in, and what type of company they may work for. Do they have kids? If so, how many? Are they married? While some of these areas may be more relevant than others knowing these things will only help you understand your target audience even more. The more you know them, the better you can serve them.

Once you can answer the general questions, you'll want to dive deeper. Think about their goals that relate to what you offer and what they want to accomplish. How can your product or service solve a problem? Are they searching for a new leather bag for a business trip? Is their child suffering from dry skin? Could they be trying to save money by learning how to maintain their pool? The possibilities are endless, and the solutions you can offer are infinite.

The next area you want to get clear on is their challenges. What keeps them up at night? What is hindering them from accomplishing their goal, and how can your product or service eliminate that challenge? Remember, your product or service needs to solve a problem, and you need to be very clear about how you can solve that problem. People want to know what's in it for them, so you need to be able to communicate that with confidence.

The more you understand your target audience, the more strategic you can be about building your brand but remember it does take time. Sometimes it's going to take working with many different customers and clients to learn who your business is for and who it isn't for. Don't stress out if you don't have all of the answers right away. However, if you are already in business and you don't know who your target audience is, then think about what your current customers have in common. Do they align with the customers and clients that you actually want? If so, spend time learning more about them. Conduct surveys and ask for reviews to find out how you can serve them even more. If your current customer or client base doesn't align with the customers and clients that you want, then consider rebranding your business so you can attract the community that you desire.

Another term you may hear when someone is referring to a member of their target audience is an ideal customer or ideal client. An ideal customer is a semi-fictional representation of the "perfect" person to buy your products or services. This is based on real data you've researched about customer demographics, behavior patterns, goals, and challenges.

The goal is to learn as much as you can about them, so you can serve them and make an impact. Understanding your target audience is crucial to branding your business because they determine how your brand should look and feel, and how it should be communicated. Before we hop into how to define those areas through market research, I want to discuss brand perception.

Brand perception is the result of your customer or client's experience with your brand. If you're just starting, no worries, simply think about the things you would like people to say.
How do you want people to feel when they come in contact with your brand? What kind of experience do you want them to have? Also, consider questions like:

- What do people say after they do business with you?
- What do you want people to say when they talk to other people about your brand?
- What initial thoughts do you want them to have when they come in contact with your brand?
- Do you want them to think luxury or down to Earth?

Brand perception matters because it reflects how buyers feel about your business. Unfortunately, you don't have much control over it. Yes, how you present your brand matters, but it means nothing if people don't feel the same. Keep in mind people are entitled to their opinions; however, if you are getting consistent negative feedback in a particular area, then it should be addressed. Understanding how you want your brand to be perceived will help you conduct market research and learn more about your target audience. This valuable process will help you determine if your product or service is feasible, and you will gain insight into the strategies that are currently working.

Think about the go-to brands in your industry that offer similar if not the same products and services as you. Their brands weren't built overnight. They went through testing to figure out what works for them, and so will you. Conducting research will give you a good starting point so that you can get a better understanding of your market. The goal is for you to take your findings and apply them to your business to find the ultimate formula that produces results.

In plain terms, market research is when you conduct a study to find out more about your target audience. It's the process of gathering information about a buyer's needs and preferences. It's essential to collect, analyze, and interpret information about your target market, consumers, competitors, and industry in general.

This process will only set you up for success, and it is helpful at any stage in your business. If you're already in business and conducting market research, start in-house to learn what your customers and clients are saying about your products and services. Consider the positive and constructive feedback you get and determine what areas need to be improved in your business.

Run polls and surveys to find out what they would like to see or learn more about. The feedback is crucial, especially if they're your target audience. It should be easier to ask your audience questions because these are people who are already interested in what you have to offer. They are more likely to be honest when they're happy with their experience and want to help you improve. I'm always conducting polls in my free Facebook group, The Strategist's Corner with Briana Ross, because I value their feedback, and I know asking them questions directly will only help serve them and me more.

If you're just starting, DON'T FREAK OUT. There are still many valuable ways to learn more about your target audience and how you can serve them. The first way you can conduct market research is by visiting discussion forums online. Platforms like Quora are filled with thousands of conversations with real people about almost anything. You can even start a discussion if there's a specific area you'd like to gain more insight on.

You can also engage in relevant Facebook groups where your target audience hangs out. You can ask questions, or you can use the search tool within the group. This will allow you to see what has already been discussed around your industry. Facebook groups are fantastic because you can begin to build very valuable relationships. Only by giving value and not just selling, I have been able to make meaningful connections, meet new business friends, get new clients, and obtain new leads. Utilizing Facebook groups (whether participating in an existing one or creating your own) is a great way to establish yourself as an expert in your industry and give endless amounts of value.

Researching established brands in your industry that offer similar products and services is also really helpful because you can learn about what type of content is currently working. Be careful not to compare yourself to other brands when doing your research. It is for research purposes only! It is not an opportunity for you to copy other brands, but to get some direction on where to start when building your brand online. We often get intimidated by other brands in our industry because they're more established, and they're killing it. Remember, there's enough room for all of us, you just have to solve a problem and be able to communicate it.

 The ultimate goal is to find out as much as you can about your target audience. The more details you know, the better, because you can speak to their pain points and establish your brand as the go-to brand for their problem/need. Collecting all of this information will allow us to serve our community and build a relationship with them. To reiterate, it's not just about your products and services. There are hundreds, if not thousands, of other brands that do what you do, so you need to focus on giving value and building a relationship to set your brand apart.

Action Steps

Outline your target audience:

- Demographics:

_____
_____
_____
_____

- What does their daily life look like?

_____
_____
_____
_____
_____
_____

- What are their goals?

_____
_____
_____
_____
_____

- What are their challenges?

_____
_____
_____
_____

How do you want your brand to be perceived?

_____
_____
_____
_____

Conduct market research:

- Determine the platform where your audience is most active: _____
- What types of content do they interact with?
  _____
  _____
  _____
  _____

- What are three things they're struggling with?
  1. _____
     _____
     _____
  2. _____
     _____
     _____
  3. _____
     _____
     _____

- What are three of their goals?
  1. _____
     _____
     _____
  2. _____
     _____
     _____
  3. _____
     _____
     _____

PART THREE

Who Is Your Brand For?

Having a clear Brand Identity is crucial for attracting your target audience. You need to be able to confidently articulate who you are, what you do, and how to talk about it. Having a business in an area you're passionate about will make things a lot easier because your brand values will align with those of your target audience. You'll have a clearer idea of how to communicate with them, and most importantly, you will understand what they're going through and what you would want to help them with.

Think about their core values and identify how they align with yours. What do you have in common, and when you were in their shoes? How did that make you feel? What do you wish you had at the time? Answering these questions will help you identify ways to create a relationship with your audience as well as your brand. It's about solving a problem and providing a solution to a problem that people are having.

One thing to always remember is there's enough room for your business. We have a tendency to feel intimidated by how many companies are already in the industry, and I have to agree, it can feel daunting at times. It's about solving a problem and presenting it uniquely. Let's be real; no one is inventing the wheel. It is all about standing out. Creating an avenue of two-way communication is the perfect way to start standing out. Create a brand that's for them and one they can count on. A brand that solves a problem sticks to its word, values its audience's opinions, and goes above and beyond to provide a fantastic customer experience. If you keep those areas in mind, I promise you will never be steered wrong.

When building our businesses, we tend to focus too much on promoting our services and booking people. We have to plant seeds first, so focus on the results that your product or service can provide. In this section, we're going to focus on how to communicate with your target audience.

Brand Positioning

Brand positioning is all about setting your brand apart from other brands. When starting or scaling your business, consider what is missing in your industry, and how you can fill the gap. Positioning your brand the right way can translate into customer loyalty, social proof, and the consumer's willingness to buy.

When positioning your brand, it's essential to use the right verbiage to attract your target audience. For example, if you have an all-natural skincare line, you may consider words like vegan, exclusive, and revive. If you have a consulting business, you may choose to use words like innovative, results-driven, and strategic. Think outside of the box when communicating your brand and focus on carrying those words out in every aspect of your business.

To position your brand uniquely, you'll want to be clear on what your audience wants, what type of experience your brand can provide, and how other brands in your industry are positioning themselves. This is going to make it a lot easier to place your brand in a way that stands out. No, this isn't a competition, but you need to know what other brands are doing so you don't do the same things.

Frequently, we get so caught up in the trends and what other brands are doing, and we end up doing the one thing we don't want to do; blend in. Don't underestimate your ideas. You may think some of your senses are out of the box or crazy, but it just may be what your industry needs. Don't be afraid to take it up a notch. Think about how you can build a relationship with your audience, take them along for the journey, and give them value.

Once you're clear on your market and what your brand is capable of, you need to come up with a brand positioning statement. To create the perfect brand statement, you want to be sure that it resonates with your audience. Think about their values and what's important to them. How can you speak to their emotional side?

Again, make sure your brand position statement aligns with what your business is capable of. For example, don't say you have fast shipping if your average order processing time is five business days.

Consider the ingredients you use or your method for creating your product. Maybe your process is a lot faster than other businesses in your industry. Perhaps your process is a lot more detailed than other brands. Dig deep to figure out what currently sets your brand apart, or how you can set your brand apart.

When you understand what makes your brand different from all of the rest, you can confidently communicate that to your audience and establish yourself as an expert. When I first launched HelloBriana Consulting, I was all over the place and ended up blending in with the thousands of other coaches and consultants. Once I realized I offer fantastic customer service, I pay attention to detail, and I help my clients get amazing results; I became more confident in what I do and who I am. Because I don't just design graphics, I help you get clear on your brand strategy as a whole. Over time I began to notice my brand position was where it needed to be when my clients and audience came to know my brand as professional, prompt, action-driven.

Action Steps

Pick three adjectives to describe your brand:

1. _____
2. _____
3. _____

Identify one thing that seems to be missing in your industry?

_____
_____
_____
_____

Identify three things you do differently from other brands:

1. _____
_____
_____
_____
2. _____
_____
_____
_____
3. _____
_____
_____
_____

Your Brand Story

Now that you have clearly defined your brand values, outlined your target audience, and understand how your brand should be positioned, it's time to determine how you can communicate value to your audience while building a relationship. The perfect way to do that is by crafting and sharing your brand story.

Your brand story is a narrative that captures facts, values, and feelings about your business. It is meant to help you connect with your audience and speak to their emotional side. Marketing has changed. There's a lot more competition so you can't just tell people to buy your products and services and expect them to buy it. You have to build your know, like, and trust factor, and show them what sets your brand apart from other brands.

The reason storytelling is so compelling is that it triggers a biological response. A good brand story grabs your attention, provokes emotion, and takes your audience on a journey. Having a strong brand story comes down to how well someone can identify with the character in the story, so be sure to consider your target audience's background, challenges, and roadblocks.

Whether you're a product or service-based business, your brand story is still equally relevant. It is a great way to build a connection with them, show them how relatable your brand is, and show them how you've gone the extra mile to meet their needs.

It is ok to have multiple brand stories, but they all need to have a character, conflict, and resolution. Larger companies have numerous brand stories that align with the same values because their target audiences are so large, and their ideal customers differ in small ways.

When you start outlining your brand story, the first area you want to describe is your character. Who is the main character of your story? Your main character can be you, a past customer or client, or someone you know. If you are not the character of your brand story, then you'll want to choose someone you can interview so you can understand their perspective on how best to connect with them. You'll also want to make sure that the main character of your story has experienced the results of your product or service to ensure you can deliver the results that your target audience is seeking. Later in this guide, we'll discuss ways you can do this, whether you're already in business or just starting.

The next area you need to outline is conflict. Think about a time when you or someone you know was in your target audience's shoes. Having a clear conflict that resonates with your target audience is crucial because it lets them know they are not alone. You are also setting the stage for the third step of creating your brand story, your resolution.

When I started being transparent about my journey as a woman and entrepreneur, I noticed a massive shift in my business. I started booking my soulmate clients, learned more about my audience, and I was able to give fantastic value to my audience because they had opened up about their challenges with me. For so long, I thought I could build a business by hiding behind it and not being the face of my brand, but instead, I was all over the place, and I didn't feel connected to my audience. Your story matters and your story has the power to help other people heal. Show people they are not alone, and they can make it through the storm.

Once you have clearly defined the conflict of your brainstorm and outlined what your audience is struggling with, it's time to determine the last area, the resolution. This is where you explain how your character was able to find a solution that got them amazing results. Once you have shared how much your character's life has changed, you can explain how they got those amazing results through your product or service.

Everyone's story is different, and depending on your products or services; you may only share certain parts of your story. For some, your brand story may be traumatic, and for others, it may be a funny story. It depends on the problem that your product or services solve. Your brand story may even be centered around the history of your business, and how you got started. This is an excellent opportunity to express yourself and explore deeper possibilities.

Remember, you can't just ask people to buy your products and services. Having a great brand story allows you to build the know and like portion, and the content you share forms the trust aspect. Having a brand story allows your audience to get to know your business, so they can determine if your brand is the right one for them.

Action Steps

Brainstorming your Brand Story

Think about a time when you or someone you know were in the shoes of your target audience. Write about it below:

_____

_____

_____

_____

_____

_____

_____

_____

_____

_____

_____

_____

_____

_____

_____

_____

_____

_____

_____

_____

_____

_____

Outline the three main areas of your brand story:

- Characters (Include who the character is, their personality, how they look, etc.):

  _____
  _____
  _____
  _____
  _____

- Conflict:

  _____
  _____
  _____
  _____
  _____
  _____
  _____
  _____
  _____

- Resolution:

  _____
  _____
  _____
  _____
  _____
  _____
  _____
  _____
  _____

PART FOUR

Execution

Your Brand Style Guide

Your brand style guide allows you is a rulebook that explains how a business should be presented. It will enable you to pull all of your visuals together to create a visual that attracts your target audience. It includes things like your brand voice, logo, colors, and more. Also, it is a reference tool that you can provide to your team to help them get a better understanding of how your brand should look and feel. Using your brand style guide will ensure that your branding is cohesive across all platforms regardless of who is working on content for your brand.

Before creating your brand's style guide, get some inspiration to help you get a handle on the million and one ideas you have. When working on the inspiration for your brand, be sure to think like your audience. After all, although this may be something you're passionate about, it's still about solving a problem for your community. Also, be sure to get feedback from others. Ask the individuals who fit in your target audience what they think of your ideas and what suggestions they can give. This allows you to get fresh eyes and determine if you're headed in the right direction or not. Just make sure the feedback you're getting is from people who fit your target audience or understand your target audience.

Once you've collected your inspiration, and you have a clearer idea of how you want your brand to look and feel, it's time to start creating your style guide. When creating your style guide, I always recommend creating a brand board to help you keep everything cohesive and organized. When beginning to work with new clients on visual branding, I always yet have them create a Pinterest board for their brand. This is where they can add any and everything they feel that adds to how they want their brand to look and feel. They can add pictures, color palettes, phrases, and more. Their Pinterest board helps me get an understanding of what they're looking for when it comes to their visual branding. I recommend doing the same thing to get inspiration and figure out how you want your brand to look. We've all heard, 'a picture is worth a thousand words,' so we want to make sure our visual branding speaks to our specific audience. Having pictures will allow you to get a clearer idea of how you want your brand to be presented, and it will make things easier when you start designing your brand elements or hire a designer to do it.

The first area of your style guide is an area we've already outlined, which is your brand story. Your brand story will help whoever is working on your content to understand the story behind your brand and get a better understanding of who your target audience is.

The next area you want to include is your brand voice. Your brand voice is how you convey your brand's personality to your audience. It can be formal or informal, but you want to make sure it aligns with your target audience's communication style and doesn't turn them off. Consider doing as much research as possible to find out how your audience communicates on social media. If you offer professional services, you may decide to go with a more formal but conversational tone. However, if you have a product-based business like a date night subscription box, you might decide to use informal verbiage.

Your brand voice isn't just the audio; it's the personality of your brand. Your brand voice then expands into its values, vocabulary, characteristics, and more! Think about the words that would define your brand's personality. Would you use words like friendly, inspiring, or informative? No matter what, make sure it aligns with your target audience, and it is a personality that resonates. Whatever you do be careful not to sound robotic, you need to be approachable and likable.

Your brand voice will be communicated through your website, social media posts, emails, blogs, and anywhere else, your brand is communicating with your audience. Having a reliable brand voice and personality allows you to connect with your audience on a personal and consistent level. It makes your brand more approachable, and your audience will be more likely to open up about the problems they are having and how your brand can assist.

In your style guide, the brand's identity is the next area you'll want to outline. You'll want to revisit questions like:

- Why did the business start?
- What are the business's beliefs?
- What separates your brand from others?

Think about the key adjectives you chose in the Brand Positioning section in Part III to describe your brand. Those adjectives will help you and whoever else you are working with, understand your brand's background of the and what makes it unique. To expand on how you want your customers to feel when they come in contact with your brand, outline three words you want your customers to use when describing your brand.

Now that your brand is transitioning into the design, you have to make sure everything is appropriately conveyed visually. Many elements play into the visual aspect of your brand, such as colors, shapes, fonts, so it's essential to identify a few overall styles for your brand to help keep things cohesive. There are many different styles to choose from, but some of the main ones include classic, quirky, vintage, and modern. Don't hesitate to do some research at any given point if you're feeling unsure about your choices, but also understand you don't have to limit yourself. Pick whichever style(s) you love and believe will attract your target audience.

Now it's time to choose your brand colors. However, don't just choose the colors you like. Instead, research your target audience to find out what they're interested in, and be sure to study color psychology. What many don't realize is specific colors evoke certain emotions, so you want to make sure your brand colors align with how you want people to feel when they come in contact with your brand. Don't be afraid to play around with different color combinations and shades. When choosing your brand color palette, be sure to stick with it. Your brand colors should be used in your logo, social media graphics, website, brochures, and any other branded items.

When I first launched HelloBriana Consulting, I had different brand colors from what I have now. They were colors that I liked but didn't attract my target audience. If you had told me one of my brand colors would be pink, I would have laughed at you because I was never a fan of the color pink. However, once I realized it was a color that resonated with my audience, I didn't have a choice but to change it. Not only did my brand begin to stand out more to my audience, but the color pink started to grow on me!

Color psychology, also known as color theory, is the study of colors and how they persuade and influence people. Different colors have different meanings and are used among specific target audiences.

Let's go through colors and what they mean. Keep in mind that each color has an array of hues that could be used, so be sure to do additional research and testing to make sure you choose the right shade.

Red is the color of drama and passion. It can be used to create a sense of urgency, stimulate, and draw attention.

Pink is a color used to convey love, compassion, and sensitivity. It is also associated with femininity and tranquility.

Orange is used to stimulate, draw attention, communicate fun, motivate, encourage, and so much more.

Yellow gives hope. It conveys fresh energy, success, and confidence. With it being the color of sunshine, it is an uplifting color that can evoke feelings of confidence.

Green creates a feeling of stability, balance, growth, and safety. It expresses renewal and life, creating a tranquil feel.

Black is the color of power, authority, and elegance. Black is an intense color that can create a sexy or secretive feel.

Blue is the color of trust. With it being the color of the sea and sky, it is believed to have a calming and soothing effect.

Purple is the color of spirituality and inspires self-awareness. It is also associated with royalty, high quality, and luxury.

These are high-level overviews of each color as you begin to explore specific shades of colors I recommend diving in deeper to the meaning of that particular shade. Be sure to do your research and choose colors based on what attracts your target audience. Don't be afraid to try different color combinations to see what works best for your brand.

The next area you'll want to include is your logo variations. Depending on your background, you may be capable of designing your logo. However, if this is something you're not comfortable with, then many graphic designers may be able to assist. Your logo will often include your business name, sometimes with or without a symbol. A well-designed logo will capture your audience's attention and tell them about your business.

Your logo will be placed in many areas, for example, your website, t-shirts, table cloths, tissue paper, etc.

Make sure that your logo looks well no matter what size it is. Your logo can help your brand stand out and make a great first impression. It should be unique, memorable, and timeless.

Your brand fonts are next. The fonts you use for your brand are essential because they will be seen anywhere your brand is noticed. Choose fonts that stand out and align with your brand. Your brand fonts help create consistency and look professional. Note, you can choose more than one font. You'll want to select a few different fonts or font combinations to use for different occasions. In your style guide, you can explain which fonts are used for what.

The last area you'll want to include in your brand style guide is your photography style with different examples. Photographers have different styles, so it is vital to choose a photographer that understands yours. Having a brand photography style is very helpful when working with visual creatives for your branding, such as photographers, graphic designers, and web designers.

I know it is a lot of information to be included in your brand style guide, but you only need to include the areas that are relevant for your brand.

Some style guides are only one sheet while others are over 100 pages; it solely depends on your brand. Remember, nothing is set in stone, so don't be afraid to make changes to your style guide if you're feeling called to.

Action Steps

Describe your brand's personality and voice:

_____
_____
_____
_____
_____
_____
_____
_____

Research the meaning of your current brand colors or the colors you have in mind for your brand, and determine if they are good fits for your brand and industry. Take notes below:

_____
_____
_____
_____
_____
_____

Choose two to three colors combinations (FREE Template in resources section)

Create a brand board on Pinterest for your brand. (Example in resources section)

Get your logo designed:

- Will you design your logo? _____
- If so, what platform will you use to design it?
  _____
- If not, who will design your logo?
  _____
- How much will it cost? _____
- What is the turnaround time? _____

Outline your brand style guide. Create a PDF yourself going over everything, or work with a graphic designer to create one. (Example in the resources section)

Website Design

Many ask when is the right time to get a website. It ranges for various businesses, but I will say this, you don't have to have a website to start building your business. Yes, having a website can make things A LOT easier; however, if you don't know how to build a website and you don't have the budget to hire a designer, then focus on income-generating activities.

I view having a website as a luxury. When I first launched my business, I was unable to get a website right away because I didn't have a budget. Thankfully, I had started blogs on Wordpress years ago, so learning website design was not a challenge for me. I chose to build my website on the platform Squarespace because it had high-end templates, drag and drop design features, and fantastic tech support and resources.

Whether you build a website yourself or hire a web designer, you need to make sure you choose the right platform for your website. Different platforms have different features and strengths, so it's essential to choose the right platform. Make sure you have a clear idea of what you need your website to be able to do, how you want it to look and feel, and what content you'll need to bring your website to life.

Top web design platforms include Wix, Wordpress, Squarespace, Shopify, and Weebly. I recommend doing research and picking the platform that you believe will best suit your business, then find a web designer that builds on that platform. Be sure to check out their website and portfolio to determine if their design style fits what you're looking for. If you decide to build your website yourself, be sure to check out that platform's resources, YouTube videos, and forums to create a branded and full-functioning website. Also, keep in mind many web designers have resources available, including, but not limited to, online courses, blogs, and one-on-one services to teach you how to build your website.

Web design is an investment of your time or money. Your lifestyle may dictate your choice. Your website should not just sit there and look pretty. It should aim to convert visitors into leads or buyers. The goal of your website should be centered around getting a return on your investment, automating your systems, and making it easier to serve your audience.

Regardless if you build your website yourself or hire a web designer, these are the pages I recommend your website should have:

Homepage: This is probably the most critical page of your website because this is what most visitors will see first. Your homepage needs to capture your visitor's attention and explain who you are and who you serve. Think about when you're surfing the internet. You only visit a page for a few seconds before going back to your search engine unless something intrigues you to read more or click. On your homepage, be sure to include who you are, what you do, who your products and services are for, and a Call-to-Action (CTA). A CTA is anything created to provoke immediate action such as a sale, option to join your mailing list or lead magnet.

About: Your about page is an opportunity for your audience to learn more about the brand and the people behind it. People want to do business with people, so getting to know the people behind the brands adds a personal touch. Your about page should include the history of your business, the founder, team members, and board members, and what sets you apart from other brands. Also, be sure to include any achievements you have received.

Frequently Asked Questions (FAQ): Having a Frequently Asked Questions page can be super helpful for visitors. It'll help them learn everything they need to know before purchasing from your business. This page will save you a lot of time from having to answer the same questions over and over again. Be sure to include the questions you get asked consistently. These questions should help remove any doubt and improve your visitor feel confident in doing business with you.

Services: This is where you'll include all of the details about any services you offer. If you are a service-based business, then you may decide to list the prices of your packages with a payment option, or you may direct people to book a consultation. When describing your services online, it's important to focus on the transformation that your service will bring. You need to be able to communicate the value in what you offer. Include details of the results potential clients can expect, what your services include, what is like working with your brand (even include testimonials if you'd like), and a CTA for them to book services or book a consultation.

Products: If you are a product-based business or a service-based business that offers a physical good, then you'll need a product page. Be sure to include all product details, including descriptions, size, ingredients (if necessary), or directions. Make it as easy as possible for visitors to buy by including an ADD TO CART button for them to easily purchase your products.

Contact: Allow visitors to contact your business whether they have additional questions about products or services, need information about their order, or inquire about partnerships. Include a simple form of collecting their name, number, email address, message, or any other information you'd like to receive. Be sure to include your business contact information. This may include your phone number, fax number, email address, and address (physical or mailing). You may even decide to include this information in the footer section of your website, so it is visible on every page. Lastly, you'll want to include information about your response time. Whether it's within 24 hours or 48 hours, it's essential to set expectations.

Blog: Having a blog can be very beneficial to your business. A blog is a section of your website that includes journal entries on topics relevant to your brand and industry. When we think about the technicalities of blogging, it is a great way to keep your website updated. You see, the more pages your website has, the better chances it has in appearing in search engines like Google, Yahoo, and Bing, especially if your blog posts are centered around similar topics. Think of your blog as a marketing tool. It is a great way to share your expertise, generate leads, and engage your audience. Your blog will also give your company a voice, and it can help your brand become more personal. We will talk more about blogging later in this guide, including how it can benefit your brand and how to generate blog topic ideas.

Press/Latest News: This page is meant to shed light on all of your brand's features. You can share any article written about your business, press releases, video features, and more. If you're a speaker or workshop facilitator, then this is a great page to mention your past speaking engagements. Be sure to include your media kit, press kit, and links to your speaking. You can also add an intake form where people can inquire about booking or featuring you.

Reviews/Testimonials: Social proof matters! People want to know that you're a trusted brand, and being able to hear from real people can help them build confidence in your brand. If you're just starting with no customers or clients, don't worry. Later in this guide, we'll discuss ways to get testimonials and reviews when you're just starting. Your review page is a great way to showcase the positive reviews your business has received. If possible, include a picture or name linked to their social media account, this will show that real people are purchasing your products and services.

Privacy Policy: A Privacy Policy is a MUST for a website. Your privacy policy lets people know what you plan to do with their information. It also allows visitors to know if their information will be shared with third parties. Make sure you're honest about your privacy policy and make sure you adhere to it.

PAGE NOT FOUND: Your Page Not Found page is also known as the "404 error" page. Visitors are directed to this page when a page no longer exists, has been moved, or it has expired. Many websites will come with a set template for this page, but if possible, edit the page and add a call to action to redirect traffic.

Terms & Conditions: Your Terms & Conditions are very similar to your privacy policy, but instead of it protecting your visitors, it protects your brand. On this page, you'll want to include any copyright, trademark, or intellectual property disclosures. Think of this page as the page that spells out the rules to your visitors.

Action Steps

Find three to five websites that have the look and feel that you like:

_____
_____
_____
_____
_____

Research graphic designers to build your website, or research platforms so you can build it yourself

Who would you like to build your website?

_____
_____

What platform will your website be built on?

_____

Outline your website pages

_____
_____
_____
_____
_____
_____
_____
_____
_____
_____
_____

Creating Compelling Content

It's time to pull everything together and start creating content now that you understand your market and audience, you know how you want and need to connect with your audience, and you have created your brand style guide. Content is the information you share directed to your audience, including social media posts, emails, blog posts, and videos. The goal is to create content that resonates with your audience so that they will know, like, and trust your brand and buy your products or services.

Think about the market research you've done. What types of questions is your target audience asking? What platform do they seem to be most active on? What topics do they seem most interested in? These questions are going to help you dive deep and create content that speaks directly to your audience. If it doesn't serve your audience, then it isn't relevant. Whenever I create content, I ask myself if it's something my target audience will value. If I'm unsure, I create polls to get their feedback.

Content is king, so being able to create content with a purpose and message is a great way to build a relationship with your audience and simply start the conversation. The world is constantly changing, and new information is always released, so it's important to stay on top of industry news. Not only does this allow you to give value to your audience and keep them in the loop, but it also keeps you sharp and in the know when it comes to making the right decisions for your business. It sounds like a lot, but try to read about your industry as often as possible by downloading apps, subscribing to blogs, or following relevant social media profiles.

When creating content online, be sure to have a clear brand voice that can connect with your target audience. Having multiple brand voices can be confusing because it lacks consistency, and it makes it harder for people to communicate with it. Remember, there are hundreds if not thousands of other people and brands covering similar topics as you, and the perfect way to stand out is by using your voice.

Keep your target audience at the forefront of your brain when creating content. The content you create should be based on the things they care about and can benefit from. Don't be afraid to get creative. Once you know your target audience, you can create content in a broader spectrum that not only informs them but can also entertain them.

When creating content, be sure to offer solutions. You're the expert, and you have a lot of knowledge, but you have to remember what is common knowledge to you may not be common knowledge to your target audience. Don't just throw facts at them. Let me know why these things matter and give them action steps they can implement.

Action Steps

Elaborate on how you can serve your audience:

_____
_____
_____
_____
_____
_____

Conduct a brain dump! Spend 10 to 15 minutes thinking only about content topics, and write everything that comes to mind. Remove any topics that don't align with the goals and challenges of your target audience.

_____
_____
_____
_____
_____
_____
_____
_____

With the list you have, begin planning content to share to your email list, blog, and social media.

Elaborate on what you would like your brand to be known for:

_____
_____
_____

Content Marketing

Content marketing is a marketing approach that focuses on creating and distributing content to a targeted audience online. Your content needs to be three things; valuable, relevant, and consistent. Creating valuable content is crucial to being able to connect with your audience online. This is how they will come to know, like, and trust your brand. Content creation is all about connecting with your community and creating a two-way communication street between your brand and your audience.

When choosing to use a content marketing approach for your business, remember this is a content-driven approach. It's about sharing your expertise, connecting with your audience, and serving them. You have to be ready to be consistent in showing up. Be consistent in your message, and be flexible to serve your audience and follow your purpose continuously.

Utilizing content marketing strategies have allowed me to build my brand in ways I could only have dreamed of. I got consistent in my message, confident in what I do, and I focused on serving my audience and giving value. There are many types of content you can share to market your brand, but in this guide, we're going to focus on methods that my clients and I have personally used. Keep in mind content creation is the actual content that serves, and content marketing is the distribution and marketing of that content. Content marketing can help you build brand awareness, build your mailing list, help you generate sales, and so much more!

Social Media Content: When it comes to content marketing, most people think of social media first, so we'll start there. Social media allows you to distribute your content across multiple channels to get your message out to the masses and either find your target audience or engage with them. Social media amplifies your brand's reach and allows you to get in front of many more people than you would doing footwork on a day to day basis. Now, this doesn't mean that you shouldn't be out there networking, but you should use it to help you get in front of more people. Social media includes, but is not limited to: Facebook, Instagram, Snapchat, Twitter, LinkedIn, Tumblr, and so many other platforms.

When deciding to use social media to build your brand, I recommend picking one platform, then adding on additional platforms as your brand grows, and you find your consistency on that platform. One of the biggest concerns I hear from my audience is how hard it is to keep up with all of the different social media platforms. The good thing is, you don't have to!

When I first started my business, I was trying to post on three to four platforms a day. I was burnt out, inconsistent, and annoyed because I didn't see results from social media. I took a step back and began to analyze the different platforms and what type of engagement I was getting. From there, I decided to focus on Facebook because it was the platform I spent the most time on, and I was gaining pretty good traction. I still posted on Instagram, but I no longer felt pressured or overwhelmed by social media. This changed the game for me, and I was able to grow my following, start my Facebook group, book amazing clients, and get many referrals. Once I felt comfortable with my consistency on Facebook, I began to focus on incorporating Instagram, and now I am working on utilizing LinkedIn more.

The key is to find out what works for you. Think about where you currently are when it comes to social media. Are you overwhelmed? Do you have a plan? If you can pick one platform to focus your efforts on, where would it be? That doesn't mean stop posting on platforms, but rather focus on growing one platform at a time. As an entrepreneur, especially a "solopreneur," it can be so easy to get overwhelmed when you're doing things alone. Because you're trying to do so many things at once, no area is getting your full attention, which means you're not getting results. Pick a starting place and expand from there.

Ebooks: As I mentioned earlier in this guide, when I first started my business, I was not just focusing on Branding; in fact, I was all over the place. I had only done a Facebook live sharing ways to get started monetizing your hobbies. I got fantastic feedback and so many questions, so I decided to create an Ebook called 6 Steps to Monetize Your Hobby (this short guide is still available on my website if you need it). I would then use this tool as a way to build my mailing list. I created this ebook with no marketing budget, and I simply wanted to help people in my community. With organic promotion on Facebook, I was able to grow my mailing list by almost 100 subscribers. This isn't a huge number, but with no marketing budget, promoting the ebook a few times a week, and less than a year in business, I was more than happy with those results. I finally had an email list I could begin to serve and build a relationship with.

As you can see, ebooks are great ways to offer free content to build your mailing list. I can only imagine what type of results I could have gotten if I would have invested in Facebook ads, but I learned a lot that has been able to help me get amazing results today. Ebooks are used as a lead generation tool to help you connect with your audience on a more personal level. Once you have spent some time online engaging with your audience, you can begin creating more in-depth content to help them get better results. You give them something free i.e., your ebook in exchange for their name, email address, and phone number.

If you decide to create an ebook for a lead generator, be sure to create a landing page that shares information on what your ebook is about, who it is for, what people are saying about it, and a form for them to opt-in and download your ebook. Later in this guide, we'll discuss email marketing a little more in-depth, along with what types of content you should be sharing with your mailing list after they have opted in and received their freebie.

Blog Posts: I hate to admit it, but I honestly don't see enough small business owners and entrepreneurs blogging. In the next part of this book, we're going to discuss precisely how blogging will build your brand online, but right now, I want to touch on the content creation side of things. When I talk to my audience about blogging the first thing they ask is what should they blog about. The answer is simple, blog about your brand, the services you offer and what sets your brand apart, or write a step by step guide. For example, if you're a makeup artist, you may decide to blog about skin regimens for different types of skin. If you're a personal trainer, you may choose to blog about why nutrition is more important than working out. If you're a graphic designer, then you may decide to blog about the benefits of working with a skilled graphic designer.

No matter what you decide to blog about, remember to give value. Still, struggling to come up with blog topics? Think about some of the frequently asked questions you get. Each of those questions can be expanded into their blog posts. Whether you've done videos or social media posts, most of your content can be repurposed into a blog post, so think outside of the box. You can also generate leads with blogging, so be sure to include a call-to-action in your blog posts by inviting people to join your mailing list or download your freebie. This then gives you another way to build your mailing list, and be able to serve your audience even more.

Blogging is a great way to connect with people. It allows them to learn more about your brand, how you can serve them, and they get a feel for your brand's voice and personality. You can even allow comments and allow visitors to give feedback and ask additional questions. Blogging also allows you to establish your brand as an expert in your industry.

PDFs: Offering workbooks, templates, and checklists are my personal favorites because it not only allows me to give a massive amount of value to my audience but they also get actionable steps they can implement immediately. If you're a service-based business owner, then offering these types of resources allows you to shed light on the problems that your products and services can help solve. This allows your audience to see some of your frameworks, and determine if they're capable of putting the work in before working with you.

When deciding to build your brand online and offer resources, it's essential to have a clear plan of action with clear goals to measure your marketing efforts. Study analytics across all of the platforms you are using, including your blogs, landing pages, and social media posts to determine what is working and what you can improve on. Remember, each platform has a different set of analytics, so be sure to spend some time understanding all of the platforms you use so you can be strategic.

Content marketing goes beyond just creating content; it dives into how you will distribute the content and how you will generate leads and sales. Create content schedules outlining when you'll post your content and where you'll post it to help you stay consistent. If you're going to launch a workbook, ebook, or start blogging, be sure to outline your promotion schedules.

Action Steps

Pick one or two social media platforms to focus on.

_____

_____

Set goals for your social media marketing efforts. How do you want social media to help you build your business? What are you wanting to accomplish with it?

- _____

- _____

- _____

- _____

Brainstorm up to three freebies that you can offer to build your mailing list. Include what freebies topic, the type of content will it be, launch date, and how it will help your audience.

1. _____

_____

2. _____

_____

3. _____

_____

Repurposing Your Content

You are going to hear me say this multiple times in this guide, but the formula isn't that complicated. We have literally been overthinking things for way too long, and I want to help you simplify things and get an actionable plan in place. Repurposing content has helped me out a lot. I'm going to be honest, sometimes I don't know what to post about or write about, so I go check out my old blog posts, emails to my mailing list from a year ago, or go through old workbooks to find content topics.

Repurposing your content is when you take a piece of content on one platform like a social media post, then you change it into another type of content and expand it on a blog post. It is simply finding new ways to recycle the content you currently have. This is the perfect way to bring life to content that's been sitting around for a while. Repurposing content can save you a lot of time because you already have the topic and framework. Now, you have to fill in the new details.

Repurposing your content reinforces your message, creating consistency in your branding. Repetition is vital for getting your message to sink in, and when your audience sees your content in multiple forms, it helps them learn. This also enables you to establish your brand as an expert in your industry. Creating content in a variety of places in a variety of formats around a single topic can help raise your profile in your industry. Reusing content also allows your content to get in front of a new audience. Sometimes when you post things the first time around, it doesn't reach your entire audience.

When deciding to repurpose your content, the first place I recommend looking is your blog, if you have one. Review old blog posts and determine which posts are still relevant now. Timeless content is referred to as evergreen content. These topics will never get old and can always be repurposed. When going through past blog posts, be sure to check your website analytics to identify your best performing posts. These are the perfect topics because you know these are topics your audience is interested in. If you see a blog post that no longer aligns with your perspective or there is an update on the subject, don't be afraid to blog about the topic again and maybe even expand on it.

There are hundreds of ways you can repurpose your content, so don't be afraid to think outside of the box. I have been able to create blog posts, courses, ebooks, and more because of repurposed content. One of the first things I did to get my brand out there was created an email challenge. A few months after running the challenge, I decided to turn the content into a workbook that I was able to offer at events that I spoke at. I have turned numerous training videos into blog posts, and believe it or not; this book is a series of blog posts, videos, courses, and other forms of content repurposed into one.

Remember, things don't have to be complicated. If you're struggling to come up with new content topics, then take a look at the content that you've already created. If you don't have a blog, consider expanding on social media posts, or turning a video into a blog post.

Action Steps

Identify three of your best performing blog posts or social media posts. Include the type of content it is (i.e. social media post, blog post, video, or caption only), and what kind of feedback you received from your audience.

1. _____
   _____
   _____
2. _____
   _____
   _____
3. _____
   _____
   _____

Determine three ways you can repurpose your content.

1. _____
   _____
2. _____
   _____
3. _____
   _____

Create a timeline to hold you accountable when it comes to creating new content.

With your current lifestyle how often can you dedicate to blogging and posting on social media? _____
_____

How soon can you begin posting on social media and blogging consistently? Pick a date, and stick to it. _____

Why haven't you been consistent in posting? If you don't have a blog, why don't you have one? If you have a blog, why aren't you consistent with it?

_____
_____
_____
_____
_____
_____
_____
_____
_____
_____

What are you going to do differently this time around to ensure that you are consistent?

_____
_____
_____
_____
_____
_____
_____
_____

PART FIVE

Ways to Build Your Brand

Once you start putting content out there and building your audience you start to get a better idea of what works and what doesn't work for your business. You can't build a business without trial and error, so expect things not to always go as planned and be flexible. Building your brand won't always be easy, but hopefully it will always be worth it for you. If you focus on serving your audience you will be able to build a relationship with them, and they will let you know what you need to do to serve them more. Don't be afraid to post polls and surveys to get their feedback. Feedback is crucial. When you have an audience that is willing to participate and give feedback it's important to nurture that.

During the early stages of my business I learned how important it is to be strategic and intentional. Having a strategy gives you the game plan to help you achieve your vision, so it's very important to have a clear vision and plan. When I started focusing on having a strategy I was able to duplicate results in my business and get more consistent results.

In this part of the guide we're going to focus on actual ways to build your brand both online and locally. Be prepared to step out of your comfort zone and take action.

When building your brand remember that your strategy is just that, your strategy. Yes, a coach or consultant like myself can share our strategies, but it's up to you to take what we teach and tweak it to make it work for your business.

Building Your Brand Online

I've always been a fairly friendly person, but building my brand online did not come easily. It was a lot harder for me because I didn't know how to be personal online. I always worked jobs interacting with customers face to face and over the phone in the past, so it was much easier to build rapport, in my opinion. I put a lot of pressure on myself during the beginning phases of my business; I felt like I had to be super professional. Unfortunately, I wasn't able to find my audience and connect with them. At the time, I didn't feel like my brand needed personality, and it hurt my business a lot.

I had to figure out how to be personal to build my brand in this impersonal online world. I began to engage more online, share my journey, and share my day to day life. This allowed my audience to get to know the real me and put a personality with my brand. It became a lot easier for my audience to open up to me about their goals and challenges as they realized how much we had in common. As I've said before, the online world is filled with hundreds if not thousands of brands offering the same or similar products and services, and everyone is trying to make money. It doesn't work to post about what you're selling all of the time. Focus on building a relationship with your audience and offering a solution because people need that connection.

When I was first starting, I was a part of many Facebook groups with thousands of entrepreneurs and business owners sharing their stories, wins, losses, strategies, and more. These communities taught me so much and allowed me to get to know my target audience. I was able to do market research, ask questions to get advice, share my expertise, book clients, and make new business friends. There are groups for everything, and they allow you to get connected with the right people to build your brand strategically. Through Facebook groups, I have met mentors, found business coaches, and I was able to develop my team. Remember, it's all about community, and Facebook groups have a lot to offer.

Starting my own Facebook group gave me my cool hiding place. I now have a community that wants to learn from me. This is a place where I can provide value unapologetically for people who wish to grow their businesses. My Facebook group taught me about consistency and how to show up no matter what. For six months straight, I went live every Sunday (except for maybe three), teaching my audience how to build their brands and consistency. This allowed me to hone in on my message, test out new types of content, and conduct market research. Starting your own Facebook group gives room for more personal engagement to build your know, like, and trust factor.

I have gone live on several platforms, including Facebook, Instagram, and Periscope, and doing this has allowed me to build my brand tremendously. It was nerve-wracking at first, but the more I did it, the easier it became. Going live allowed people to get to know me as a person and learn my personality. After a while, it became fun to hop on and get a chance to chat with my audience.

I first started going live on Periscope three years ago. Call me crazy, but I liked it when no one tuned in. The live was more like a practice run, and I could focus on sharing the content with no distractions. Many of us don't want to go live because we are afraid no one will tune in, or we don't want to mess up. I want to remind you that both are fine. You have to show up no matter what. Consistency is critical when it comes to building your brand online, so if no one shows up the first time, maybe try a different day or time the next time around. You could also conduct a poll to see what day and time works best for your audience. Remember, live is live, so you're going to mess up more often than never. You're human, and this allows your audience to see the real.

Remember, everything we have discussed in this guide and will discuss in the following sections are all about building a relationship with your audience to build your brand.

Branding is about the feeling you want people to have when they come in contact with your business, so taking the time to get to know them and engage with them will help your brand go a long way.

Hosting live masterclasses is a lot of fun for me because it's like an engaged Facebook live. You can either host a free masterclass to build your mailing list or charge for access. Now, you've probably heard the terms masterclass and webinar used interchangeably, but I do want to make sure you know the difference. Webinars are typically used as lead magnets to bring awareness to a problem, discuss why a solution is needed, and often have a sales pitch at the end. Masterclasses, on the other hand, usually go more into how the problem is solved and give more details along with actionable steps. Masterclasses sometimes have sales pitches at the end, but they are centered around sharing expert knowledge. I love to use a platform called Crowdcast for my masterclasses. Crowdcast makes it easy to access registration and integrate with my website. During class, Crowdcast allows you to host polls, attach documents, and have a chat to keep students engaged.

As I mentioned in the last section, blogging is a great way to get your content out there.

Blogging is one of the best ways to help generate organic traffic to your website without having to invest in marketing (although you may choose to invest in platforms like Google Adwords). Blog posts live on your site unless you delete them, and by consistently blogging, you are continually updating your website and attracting new visitors. If you don't blog, it is going to be very hard to generate traffic from search engines like Google and Yahoo, because your website doesn't have enough relevant pages or it hasn't been updated in a while. This makes the search engine think (for lack of better words) your website is outdated. When someone googles a topic, the sites that are consistently visited or updated are shown first. Search engines love being able to share relevant content to searchers.

Blog posts should give value to your audience and even make them want to share your content on social media. Having blog posts on your website also gives you consistent content you can share across your social media profiles, to your mailing list, and so much more. Your blog posts should be anywhere from 500 words and up depending on what your audience prefers. I recommend blogging at least once a week. If you're unable to commit to blogging every week, then I would highly suggest at least every two weeks.

As you can see, there are many ways to build your brand, and I hope I even sparked some new ideas for you. To build a reliable brand online, you must know your product or service like the back of your hand, know who your target audience is so you can create relevant content, and you have to do your research. The formula isn't complicated at all. We often overcomplicate things, and that's what makes it hard for us to get results in our businesses. Yes, you need to have a vision, but don't get so caught up on your vision that you start to overthink the steps you can take right now to get there. Focus on the action steps you can take now.

You have to show up, be consistent in your message and presence, and focus on solving a problem. If you do those three things, you will see results. Now, you may not see them overnight, but with your discipline and consistency, it will come.

Action Steps

Outline four ways you can build your brand online:

1. _____
_____
2. _____
_____
3. _____
_____
4. _____
_____

Outline five action steps to help you take action with each way to build your brand online:

1. _____
_____
  • _____
  _____
  • _____
  _____
  • _____
  _____
  • _____
  _____
  • _____
  _____
2. _____
_____
  • _____
  _____

- _____
  _____
- _____
  _____
- _____
  _____
- _____
  _____

3. _____
   _____
   - _____
     _____
   - _____
     _____
   - _____
     _____
   - _____
     _____
   - _____
     _____

4. _____
   _____
   - _____
     _____
   - _____
     _____
   - _____
     _____
   - _____
     _____
   - _____
     _____

Email Marketing

Email marketing is a digital marketing strategy that focuses on communicating and selling to prospects and customers via email. With an effective email marketing strategy, you can convert prospects to loyal customers. Believe it or not, email is still one of the top communication channels. Think about how many times you check your email a day. Most people check their email multiple throughout the day, so this gives you another opportunity to build relationships and nurture leads.

Email marketing, like anything else, requires consistency. I struggled with this for a while, but once I got serious about giving value to my email subscribers, I was able to create a plan and get consistent. Since then, I have been able to learn more about my audience and start monetizing my list. One of the best feelings is sending out an email to my list, and they respond with emails, answers to my surveys, and purchases.

The people who have expressed interest in your brand by opting into your mailing list are considered a warm audience. I do not recommend buying email lists or randomly adding people to your mailing list. Always make sure your subscribers are people who opted in or have told you they want to be a part of your mailing list. This will help your analytics (we'll discuss this more in a little bit).

Another great thing about email marketing is you own your mailing list. You don't ever have to worry about not being able to communicate with them. There have been a few times when social media platforms have shut down, and business owners were freaking out because that is how they made their money. Never rely solely on social media to make money in your business. Use social media as a tool to drive traffic to your website, then focus on converting them into leads, then customers or clients.

When deciding to incorporate email marketing into your brand and content strategy, it's essential to make sure you have a plan and systems in place to make sure things are running seamlessly. Email marketing platforms like MailChimp, ConvertKit, Constant Contact, and Squarespace Email Campaigns are all great platforms to start with. I recommend doing research comparing each of the platforms to ensure you pick the right platform for your business.

Once you've picked your platform, you'll want to build a landing page enticing people to join your mailing list or to grab your freebie. Your freebie a.k.a. Lead Magnet is a piece of content that you offer for free in exchange for someone's email address. Earlier in this guide, in the Content Marketing section, we discussed a few possible lead magnets, including ebooks and worksheets. Other lead magnets include resource lists, free consultations, webinars, quizzes, and coupons. As you can see, the possibilities are endless, so get creative when thinking about what kind of offer you can use to start building your mailing list. If you're an online boutique, you may decide to offer a percentage off of a purchase. If you're a personal stylist, you may choose to create a free style quiz. If you're a new coach, you may decide to offer free consultations. Don't be afraid to test out different types of freebies, or incorporate various freebies into your website.

Don't overthink your freebie. It doesn't need to be a long research paper. It should be relatively short and easily consumable for your audience. Make sure it's actionable so subscribers can take action as soon as possible, and it creates noticeable results. If you have a good freebie, then your subscribers will continue to engage with your brand and eventually make a purchase.

When building your landing page, make sure it is optimized for success. Make sure it clearly outlines who your freebie is for and what they can expect, and make it easy for visitors to opt-in. Be sure to use an enticing heading to make visitors pause to read more, and be sure to include a helpful description. Your freebie doesn't just have to appear on a specific landing page. You can use pop-up boxes, the footer menu, a blog page, and other spaces to position your opt-in form. So get creative!

If your freebie isn't getting the results that you want, then you'll want to take a look at a few areas. Make sure the freebie is relevant to what your audience needs. Frequently we offer resources because that's what we want to offer and not what our audience needs or wants. Yes, you're the expert, but listening to your audience and their needs is the key. Once people have started to opt-in to your freebie, try to get their feedback on their experience so you can make any necessary changes to make it better.

You do not have to offer a freebie to get people to join your mailing list. I do have a page on my website where you can simply join my site to stay in the loop of upcoming events, launches, blog posts, and more. However, I do offer freebies also, so I have created multiple ways for people to join my mailing list based on the type of support they need.

Email marketing is just as important as any of your other marketing efforts because it is very personal. If you haven't started building your email list yet, then I highly recommend you start. Once you get people to opt into your list, be sure to send them relevant emails that keep them updated, give value, offer products or services, or share promotions. Remember, don't overthink it. You can send emails repurposing your content, sharing blog or social media posts, or informing your audience of current events. When it comes to how often you should email your mailing list, I recommend at least once a week, but not quite every day. If you can't commit, then start at biweekly then work your way up to a week. The important thing is that you get started.

Once you are emailing your list consistently, you'll want to analyze your analytics. Of course, the dashboard will look different depending on the platform, but the central analytics you'll see are open rates and click rates. Your open rate tells you what percentage of your mailing list is opening your emails, and your click rate shares what percentage of your list is clicking the links in your emails. These numbers are crucial because if you are struggling to get subscribers to open your emails, then that tells you that you may need to work on your subject lines. If people are opening your emails but aren't clicking the links, then that tells you that you may need to tweak some things with your email content. The important thing is to know your numbers. When you know your analytics, and you understand them, you can begin to test things out to get better results.

You may wonder what all of this has to do with branding. It has everything to do with branding. Branding is how you want people to feel when they come in contact with your brand. Sending out emails allows you to incorporate your brand voice and brand colors, and adds to your overall branding. It's another avenue for you to share your expertise and position your brand as the go-to brand in your industry.

Action Steps

Research email marketing platforms and choose the best platform for your brand.

List three email marketing platforms you are interested in using:

- _____
- _____
- _____

Which platform is best for your brand?

_____

Brainstorm topics for your email list and content you already have that you could share with them:

- _____
  _____
- _____
  _____
- _____
  _____
- _____
  _____
- _____
  _____
- _____
  _____
- _____
  _____
- _____
  _____

Outline how you will build your mailing list (will you offer a freebie?) and set goals CREATE!

How will you get people to opt-in to your list?

_____

_____

If you decide to create a freebie, what type of freebie will it be?

_____

What is the topic of your freebie?

_____

_____

_____

What will people learn from your freebie?

_____

_____

_____

_____

_____

_____

_____

Building Your Brand Locally

One thing I learned early in business is you can't solely rely on social media to build your brand. It is a potent tool to help bring awareness to build your brand, but at some point, you will need to branch out and network, expand your team and do some leg work. I got tired of sitting behind my computer, building my business. It was a little tougher for me because I've always been a pretty sociable person, and I thrive off of getting the opportunity to interact with people face to face. When building your brand locally, it's essential to be intentional and make the most of your time. Focus on building relationships and offering a solution.

Meeting with people face to face allows you to build remarkable connections. People get to see your brand in action, learn your personality, and connect with you on a personal level. The online world can be so impersonal, so take advantage of opportunities to network with people in person. There are so many people out there that are willing to help you on your journey, and you may be able to help them with theirs. If they are unable to assist, then they may know someone who can assist you. The goal is to build brand awareness, make an impact, and bring value to the table. Here are a few ways that I have been able to build my brand locally.

One of the first things I did to build my brand locally was to attend networking events. I researched events in my city and tried out a few to determine what types of events my target audience was attending. At first, the thought of attending networking events was intimidating. However, once I got over myself and started going to events regardless of who was going with me, I began to meet some fantastic people.

When attending networking events, I always take my business cards and have my 30-second elevator pitch ready. Having an elevator pitch allows me to introduce myself, tell others what I do and who I serve, and depending on the situation, I mention the services and resources I offer. Write an elevator pitch if you don't have one, and practice in front of the mirror or with friends and family. With practice, you'll get better about communicating who you are and what you do. Often we miss opportunities because we are unable to communicate effectively what we do, and having an elevator pitch will allow you to stay ready.

Once I was able to start communicating who I am and what I do with confidence, I noticed a huge shift. When attending events, I was able to start making new business friends, meet new clients, and I was presented many different types of opportunities that would not have been available to me if I didn't know who I was.

The next thing I did to build my brand locally was host events. I'll be honest, hosting events and planning everything myself is a little overwhelming, however seeing the event come together is truly amazing. Hosting my events allowed me to create my own opportunities and get out of my comfort zone. I was able to get up close and personal with my target audience, ask questions, and learn how I can better serve them. During my events, I can give tons of value, and this makes it a lot easier for my audience to see that I know what I'm talking about. Events are honestly my favorite way to build my brand locally because it gives me full creative control, and I'm able to build solid relationships with people. I have learned more about who my brand is for, booked new clients, and booked speaking engagements because I have footage to post on social media.

It is so important to have a clear plan when hosting your event. No, things may not go exactly as planned, but at least you have a framework you can follow. Have a clear outline of who your event is for, what attendees will gain, and a content marketing strategy to build buzz and get attendees registered. You also need a clear agenda for your event. Outline the series of events and how long it will be, and try to stay on schedule as much as possible if you realize that you're running behind either focus on getting through the content or cut the content short. People plan out their days and fit your events into their schedule, so be sure to keep that in mind.

Collaborating with other brands is a great way to build off of each others' audience to get in front of more people. It is so important to make sure both of your brands align with one another. If you want to maximize your results at an event, your target audience must be present, and your event needs to run smoothly. There may be hiccups along the way from planning your event until the event day, but don't panic. It happens. You have to be as flexible as possible. Also, please make sure there are proper agreements in place to make sure that all parties involved have a clear understanding of their role in the event from the planning process to the event day. The agreement should also outline and have clear days for compensation or investments needed.

The third way I was able to build my brand locally is by speaking at events. This is probably the toughest of them all because it required me to take action and get out of my head. Although I'm outgoing, I was terrified to get in front of people and speak, but I always knew I had a lot of information I wanted to share. Hosting my first event allowed me to get more comfortable with the idea of speaking in front of others, so later that year, when I had my first speaking engagement, I was a little more prepared. Yes, I was very nervous, I even thought about backing out; however, I knew if I wanted to grow my brand the way I always dreamed of I had to step out and do something different. Speaking forced me to get comfortable with my message and communicating with my target audience.

When speaking at events, make sure the event aligns with your brand, and those present are your target audience. Please do your research on the brand, check out their social media content, and find out what their audience is like. It is so important not to go into events blindsided. Also, be sure that your message aligns with the attendees. The goal is to set yourself up for success, and doing your research beforehand and being prepared is a great way to do that.

Building my brand at a local level has allowed me to learn so much about business, my audience, and events. I enjoy getting to connect with people on a personal level because it is much more meaningful, and it allows people to get to know me on a personal level.

Don't be afraid to host your event or apply for that speaking engagement. Sometimes you have to reach out or create your own opportunities to start taking your business to the next level. Always remember, if you want different results, you have to do something different. It would help if you did some testing to figure out what works for you. In every experience, there's a lesson.

Action Steps

Make a list of three upcoming events you plan to attend, and stick to it.

1. _____
_____
2. _____
_____
3. _____
_____

Brainstorm ideas for events you can host:

- _____
_____
_____
- _____
_____
_____
- _____
_____
_____
- _____
_____
_____

If you decide you want to speak or build your brand as a speaker design a speaker sheet or have one designed for you.

Research events you can pitch your brand to:
_____
_____
_____

The Formula

Branding is all about how you want people to feel when they come in contact with your brand. It's about creating an experience that they will love, come back for, and tell others about. One of the best feelings is having people who believe in your message and support you along your journey. When you focus on building genuine relationships, you begin to plant seeds that will bud and grow over time, offering you blessings you won't even be able to wrap your mind around.

Entrepreneurship isn't a comfortable journey. It requires consistency, discipline, and passion. Figure out what you can commit to now and stick to it. Stop comparing your life to others, and what consistency looks like for them, because your life is completely different. When you define your consistency, you begin to operate in your own lane. Showing up on your schedule consistently allows your audience to get to know your plan, so they will know when to expect you. For example, if you know you can't go live on social media once a week, then start biweekly and be sure to give value in-between lives.

One of the easiest ways to start becoming consistent in your message and across any platform is by planning out your content.

Planning out my content has literally saved my business, and it has allowed me to become very intentional about the content I post and how I interact with my audience. If I'm feeling inspired, I will post what's on my heart, but if I'm not inspired, I have content to post anyway because I planned it out. We all have lives, so planning out your content will save you a lot of time because you're not spending time every day trying to figure out what to post.

If you're struggling to try to stay afloat running your business alone, then it's time to outsource. Many of us think we can't afford to outsource tasks in our business because we don't have the money when the money is just going somewhere else right now. You're going to have to make a sacrifice, but when you start outsourcing tasks in your business, you will become a lot more productive, and you will make more money. I know from personal experience. I was struggling and worn out in my business doing everything by myself, and I was inconsistent. One of the first areas that I outsourced to a Virtual Assistant was my blog posts and email content. I gave her access to my backend and the main points for my content, and she did the rest. Now, I have two amazing women who I have been working with to help run my business and remain consistent. Running a business is not for one person. Yes, you may start out doing things by yourself, but it's not meant to stay that way.

You can find virtual assistants with any level of experience starting at affordable rates.

If you want to build your brand online, then you have to show up consistently, but you're going to have to test out different avenues to figure out what works for your brand. There is no set way to do things just because of the type of business that you have. Your strategic plans are going to be based on your vision for your brand. That's why it's so important to have a solid foundation. Without a solid foundation for your brand, you won't know who your audience is, what types of services you need to offer, and you're going to feel all over the place and stressed out.

Get clear on what you want for your business, who you serve, and what type of impact you want to have. Then write out your goals that align with that vision. Once you have your goals, you can then break it down into monthly or weekly action steps to help you stay on track. Running a business isn't easy, so you must have a solid plan in place to keep you on track. Even if you veer off track with a plan, you can quickly get back on track.

Be sure to conduct a Brand Audit because this will allow you to get a clear idea of where your brand currently stands, whether or not you're on track, and what steps you need to take to move forward. Start where you are now and outline steps to help you obtain your goals. It's time to get real with yourself and your business and face the things you've been putting off. One of the main reasons we don't accomplish our goals is because we don't want to face the problem head-on to make the necessary changes. We often become content with where we are but complain when we don't see results. It's time to do something different. Your business can't afford to wait any longer.

Surround yourself with people who are going to push you and hold you accountable. This isn't an easy journey, and it's so important to have a strong support system to keep you grounded. If you don't know any entrepreneurs or don't have the support you need, attend networking events, and join online communities to start connecting with people. You would be surprised at how many people need and want support just like you. We're in this together, so don't be afraid to ask for help.

Branding isn't hard; it's challenging. Just remember how you want people to feel when they're introduced to your business. Focus on giving value and building relationships, and you will never go wrong. Remember, don't overthink things. In business there is a lot of trial and error, and you will make mistakes. However, it's important to view the lesson in the situation instead of beating yourself up about what happened. Focus on the positive lesson in the situation, and figure out where you went wrong, so the same thing doesn't happen again.

You can do anything you put your mind to, but you first have to believe it then get a plan in place to achieve it. The clearer your vision is, the more intentional you can be with your actions and strategy. I want to see you win, and you will win, you just have to take action.

RESOURCES

I mean it when I say I want to help you win, so I created additional resources for your to be able to implement what you're learning.

FREE RESOURCES

The Vault

Visit www.hellobrianaconsulting.com/vault , use the code FORMULA to access my FREE resource hub that contains worksheets, pdfs, ebooks, and more to help you build the brand you've always dreamed of.

The Strategist's Corner with Briana Ross

FREE Facebook group full of entrepreneurs who are taking action and building their brands. This community is full of tools, tips, and live trainings.
www.facebook.com/groups/thestrategistscorner

Business Blog

www.hellobrianaconsulting.com/blog

Instagram: HelloBriana Consulting

www.instgram.com/hellobrianaconsulting

PAID RESOURCES

The Brand It Academy

Online learning for entrepreneurs! The Brand It Academy consists of online courses entrepreneurs can take at their own pace.

www.thebranditacademy.com

Book Your Consultation

Are you ready for a one-on-one approach? Book your consultation today, so we can create an actionable plan to help you take your brand to the next level.

www.hellobrianaconsulting.com/workwithbriana

Brand Strategy Coaching

Are you confused about the next steps you need to take to build your brand? Do you need a detailed plan to help you show up everyday and serve your audience? Are you ready to build the brand you've always dreamed of and get the blueprint on how to do that? If you're ready to put in the work, then my one-on-one coaching package is perfect for you.

www.hellobrianaconsulting.com/brand-strategy

Graphic Design

Need beautiful, clean, yet impactful visual branding to help set your brand apart? I design websites, logos, packaging, labels, brochures, and more to help you properly communicate your brand's value.

www.hellobrianaconsulting.com/graphicdesign

Self-Publishing

Are you ready to share your story or expertise and establish your brand as an expert in your industry? At HelloBriana Consulting, I offer done-for-you self-publishing services to help you monetize your knowledge or story. This package includes cover design, web design, manuscript formatting, coaching sessions, and more!

www.hellobrianaconsulting.com/selfpublishing

Glossary

Brand Awareness - how well a brand is known

Brand Mission - how a business plans to impact the lives of their audience

Brand Perception - how a business is perceived based on the customer's experience

Brand Positioning - the place a brand occupies the customer's mind and how it distinguished from competitors

Brand Purpose - the reason why the business exists

Brand Strategy - a long-term plan meant to build awareness around business and build a relationship with the audience

Brand Style Guide - a rule book for a business that explains how a company is to be presented to the world through its visual branding

Brand Vision - where a business will be in the future

Brand Voice - how a business communicates with its audience; it's personality

Branding - the promotion of a company using marketing, and it's distinctive design and experience.

Content - Content is any piece of information.

Content Marketing - a marketing approach that focuses on providing valuable content online to build relationships with audiences and provoke action

Color psychology - the study of hues and their effect on human behavior

CTA - call to action; a marketing term that refers to anything designed to provoke immediate action

Demographics - statistical data relating to the populations and the groups within it

Email Marketing - a form of marketing used to communicate with the audience via email, give value and encourage them to buy

Evergreen Content - content that is relevant over time regardless of the date, and remains fresh over a long period.

Freebie - a free piece of content that you offer in exchange for someone's email address

Market Research - the study of a specific audience

ROI - Return on Investment; the ration between net profit and cost of investment

Repurposing Content - converting one piece of content into another type of content

Target Audience - who a business's product or service is intended for (often referred to as an ideal customer or ideal client)

Made in the USA
Columbia, SC
11 October 2020